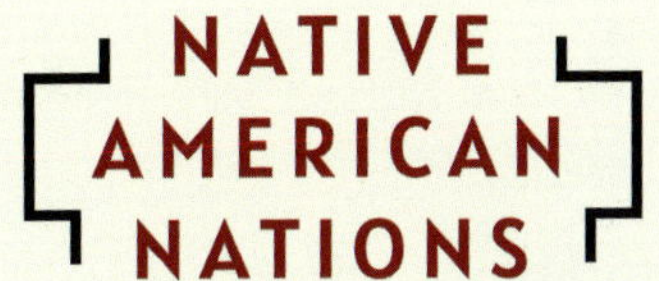

Inuit

F.A. BIRD

Checkerboard Library

An Imprint of Abdo Publishing
abdobooks.com

ABDOBOOKS.COM
Published by Abdo Publishing, a division of ABDO, PO Box 398166, Minneapolis, Minnesota 55439.

Printed in the United States of America, North Mankato, Minnesota
102024
012025

Editor: Lauri Nelson
Design: Mighty Media, Inc.

Cover Photograph: Artur Widak/NurPhoto/AP Images
Interior Photographs: Ad_hominem/Shutterstock Images, p. 7; Brown Bear/Windmil Books/Universal Images Group/Getty Images, p. 9; Chronicle/Alamy Stock Photo, p. 23; Dominik Magdziak/Getty Images, p. 27; Education Images/Universal Images Group/Getty Images, p. 5; Ivan Dmitri/Michael Ochs Archives/Getty Images, p. 19; Library and Archives Canada/Maria Spilsbury collection/e010994603, p. 25; Paolo KOCH/Gamma-Rapho/Getty Images, p. 13; Patrick Endres/Newscom, p. 29; Pictures from History/Universal Images Group/Getty Images, p. 17; SSPL/Getty Images, p. 15; Topical Press Agency/Hulton Archive/Getty Images, p. 11; Zhuravlev Andrey/Shutterstock Images, p. 21

Library of Congress Control Number: 2024938798

Publisher's Cataloging-in-Publication Data
Names: Bird, F.A., author.
Title: Inuit / by F.A. Bird
Description: Minneapolis, Minnesota : ABDO Publishing, 2025 | Series: Native American nations | Includes online resources and index.
Identifiers: ISBN 9781098296230 (lib. bdg.) | ISBN 9798384917342 (ebook)
Subjects: LCSH: Eskimos--Juvenile literature. | Inuit--Juvenile literature. | Yupik--Juvenile literature. | Native Americans--Juvenile literature. | Indians of North America--Juvenile literature. | Indigenous peoples--Social life and customs--Juvenile literature. | Cultural anthropology--Juvenile literature.
Classification: DDC 973.0497--dc23

Contents

Homelands

The Inuit (EE-neu-eet) lived across a vast area of northern lands. They lived along the coasts of Greenland and Siberia. They also lived in northern Canada and on the coast of Alaska.

Inuit homelands had long, cold winters. Winter was dark, with only a few hours of sunlight during the day. From 40 to 125 inches (100 to 320 cm) of snow fell yearly.

In some areas, a few inches of soil thawed in late spring. Many Inuit moved inland to gather berries and wild plants. They also hunted and fished in lakes and streams.

In the fall, lakes and streams froze. Many animals moved to the coast or **migrated** south. So in the winter, the Inuit moved to their coastal settlements to hunt sea animals.

The Cree were another group of native people living in northern Canada. The Cree called the Inuit *Eskimos*. The word *eskimo* means "raw meat eaters." But Inuit prefer to call themselves *Inuit*, which means "the people."

The Ilulissat ice fjord in Greenland comes from one of the most active glaciers in the world.

CHAPTER 2

Society

Inuit lived in settlements that contained a few families. A settlement could have anywhere from 40 to 100 people. Laws of expected behavior kept society in order.

Each Inuit group had its own leader. The leader was usually the eldest male. He had to understand the **migration** patterns of the animals and be able to predict weather patterns. He also had to be a skilled hunter and fisherman.

Each group also had an angatkuq (an-gat-koock). He or she was a healer, an adviser, and a spiritual person. The angatkuq performed rituals and songs to keep the people healthy. If hunters could not find game, the angatkuq performed songs and rituals to bring back the animals.

Another important person in Inuit society was the whale crew leader. Each group had a whale crew leader who organized whale hunts. He also kept the special tools needed for hunting whales.

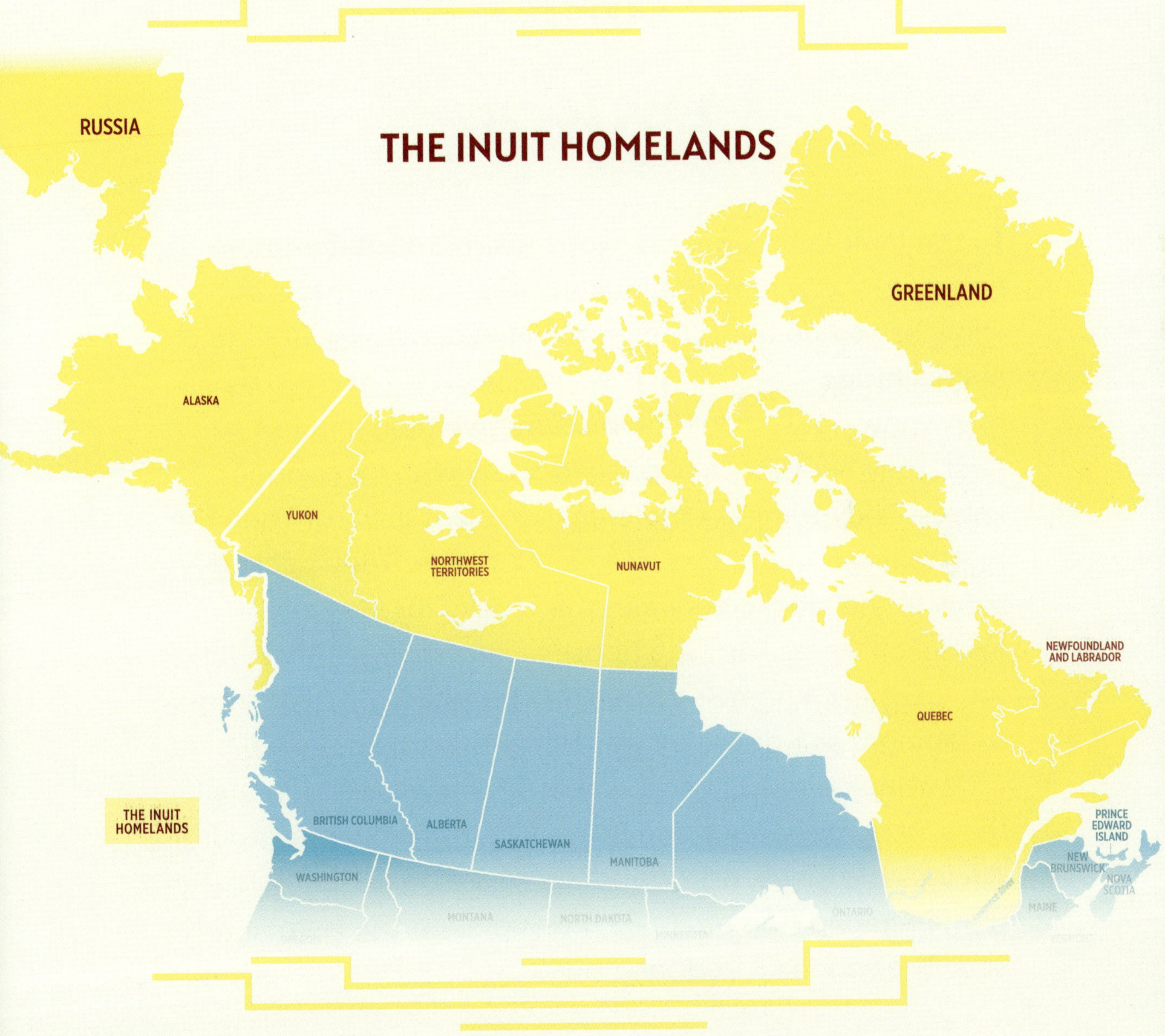

THE INUIT HOMELANDS
RUSSIA
GREENLAND
ALASKA
YUKON
NORTHWEST TERRITORIES
NUNAVUT
NEWFOUNDLAND AND LABRADOR
QUEBEC
THE INUIT HOMELANDS
BRITISH COLUMBIA
ALBERTA
SASKATCHEWAN
MANITOBA
PRINCE EDWARD ISLAND
NEW BRUNSWICK
NOVA SCOTIA
WASHINGTON
MONTANA
NORTH DAKOTA
ONTARIO
MAINE

Homes

In the Inuit language, the word *iglu* (IG-loo) means house. In the winter, the Inuit lived in houses made of snow or **sod**. In the summer, they lived in houses made of animal **hides**.

A snow house could be built by two men in a few hours. First, they cut blocks of packed snow with long, bone knives. They trimmed the blocks to slant inward. Then the men stacked the blocks, forming a dome. They packed snow in the cracks between the blocks for insulation. Inside, oil lamps kept the houses warm and bright. A long tunnel at each home's entrance prevented the heat from escaping. Each doorway was covered with an animal hide.

The Inuit also built sod homes in the winter. Men built the sod homes about one foot (30 cm) below the ground. They used stones, **driftwood**, or whale bones to build the dome-shaped frames. Then they covered the frames with sod. The sod insulated the houses.

The Inuit build snow houses as short-term shelters when they must travel long distances.

Food

Different seasons brought a variety of food to the Inuit. In the winter, the Inuit hunted seal, walrus, caribou, and whale. The Inuit **harpooned** seals and walruses from small, one-person boats called kayaks (KYE-aks). Hunting a whale required a group of men. A larger boat called an **umiak** (OO-mee-ak) was needed. When the water froze, men hunted on top of the ice. They waited by a seal's air hole to harpoon the animal when it came up to breathe.

In late spring, the Inuit gathered wild roots, grasses, and berries. The plants were eaten fresh, or dried in the sun for later use. The Inuit also hunted birds with bows and arrows. They collected the birds' eggs for food, too.

In the summer, men fished. They used hooks, nets, handwoven traps, and spears made from what they found.

The women preserved the meat and fish the men had hunted. They salted it, froze it, or dried it over a fire. Food was stored in special buildings to keep animals out.

Inuit men cut the meat from animals after a successful hunt.

CHAPTER 5

Clothing

Inuit women made clothing from the hides of caribou, seal, polar bear, and arctic fox. They sewed with **sinew** thread, and needles made from bone, antler, or walrus ivory.

In winter, the Inuit wore two sets of clothing. They wore underclothes that included shirts, pants, and socks with the fur facing inward. Over these they wore a set of outer clothes, with the fur facing outward. The outer clothes included a parka, long pants, and boots. In the summer, the Inuit wore only the underclothes, but with the fur turned outward.

The Inuit used special materials to make warm clothes. Wolverine or wolf fur was used on parka hoods. Ice does not stick to these kinds of fur. Clothing made from seal intestines was watertight and could be worn as a raincoat. Caribou or bearded seal boots were stuffed with grass. Hide mittens were worn with the fur turned inward.

Three Inuit women dressed in traditional clothing at the Northern Games in 1975.

Crafts

The Inuit were excellent carvers. They carved with **bow drills** and knives made of stone. The Inuit carved materials such as soapstone, wood, antler, and ivory.

Inuit carvings had many purposes. Sometimes the carvings decorated weapons, clothing, and handles. Other times the Inuit used ivory carvings to record their history. They carved masks to use in ceremonies. The Inuit also carved small figurines of animals, such as caribou and seals. They carried the figurines for good luck.

The Inuit were also skilled basket makers. They used baleen to make their baskets. Baleen is what hangs down from a whale's upper jaw and helps it filter out food.

Today, some Inuit men and women continue to make traditional crafts. They sell their carvings to make money. The carvings may show animals, characters from stories, or scenes from Inuit ways of life. They also sell jewelry made from baleen.

This Inuit tool set includes a thimble holder, an awl, and a sinew thread holder.

CHAPTER 7

Family

Family was important to the Inuit. Survival in harsh climates depended on the entire family working together. A family included a father, a mother, children, and grandparents. Each person in the family had a job.

Inuit men hunted and fished. Men also made tools such as **bow drills**, spears, **harpoons**, and bows and arrows. They carved hooks for fishing. The men built homes and made household goods.

Men also built dogsleds from **driftwood**. Sometimes the sled runners were made from whale bones. Men built frames for the kayaks and **umiaks**, too.

Inuit women prepared food for eating and storage. They cooked over soapstone lamps that burned **blubber** or oil. The women also prepared the animal **hides** to be made into tents, clothing, and boats. They were expert sewers. They sewed hides together so well that the hides remained waterproof.

An Inupiat family. The Inupiat are members of the Inuit culture.

Children

Inuit children were cared for by everyone in the family. The children learned by listening to stories. They learned about the dangers of living in a harsh climate, and to listen to their elders.

Boys learned how to hunt, fish, and trap. Sometimes they caught fish with a line and hook through small holes in the ice. Boys would sometimes go with the men on hunts. This way they learned how to find animals and understand weather patterns.

Girls made small tents and played with dolls. They also had storytelling knives. They used these dull knives to draw animals on the ground. Then they told stories about each drawing.

Children also played cat's cradle. They used string made of seal **sinew**. They used the string to make animal figures. They did this by moving their fingers through the string.

A young boy watches an Inuit elder so he can learn to use the bow drill.

Traditions

During the winter nights, the Inuit gathered in their homes to share the daily events and tell stories. They often told the story of "The Woman from Below the Ocean." Some Inuit call her Sedna.

A long time ago, Sedna was a human being. Her father mistreated the girl and **banished** her from camp. Then he felt bad and went to find her. She had married. When the husband was out, the father took his daughter. When the husband returned, he went looking for his missing wife.

The father was scared of the husband's anger. So, he threw his daughter out of the kayak. She hung on with her fingertips. The father cut his daughter's fingers off. Each finger that fell into the water created a marine mammal.

The daughter sank to the bottom of the ocean. As she sank, the spirits of Air and Moon saw what had happened. They gave her the power to live underwater.

Mask of Sedna, the "Guardian of the Inuit." She calms the waters and releases just enough sea mammals for the Inuit to hunt.

War

War was rare among the Inuit. The Inuit were a peaceful people. They also lived in remote areas that kept them away from other groups.

Occasionally, an Inuit group traveled into another's hunting and fishing territory. This contact sometimes resulted in a disagreement. Disagreements were often handled at gatherings.

Instead of fighting, the men would sing dueling songs. Two men would face off against each other. They would make up songs.

Some made up songs to insult the other man. Others made up funny songs. The man who made up the best song won the contest. The people laughed at the songs and soon forgot about fighting.

A singing duel was watched by the whole camp.

Contact with Europeans

Sir Martin Frobisher was one of the first European explorers to meet the Inuit. In 1576, he was looking for the Northwest Passage to Asia. In 1585, John Davis arrived among the Inuit. Today, Davis Strait is named after him.

Early European explorers traded with the Inuit. They offered guns, tools, coffee, sugar, and tea in exchange for the Inuit's kayaks, fresh meat, furs, and warm clothing.

Contact with Europeans brought problems to the Inuit. The Europeans brought diseases that killed many Inuit. The traders also killed many animals, making many species **endangered**.

Admiral Robert E. Peary also spent time with the Inuit. He studied the Inuit's clothing, food, and transportation. Peary learned how to survive in the harsh arctic climate. This helped him to discover the North Pole in 1909.

Missionaries first came to the Inuit at Nain, Labrador, Canada, in 1771.

Susan Aglukark

Susan Aglukark is an Inuit singer and songwriter. She was raised in Arviat. It is a small community in Canada's Northwest Territories.

Aglukark's music mixes beautiful Inuit chants with the sounds of pop music. She sings both in English and her native language, Inuktitut (EE-nook-tee-toot). Aglukark's music joins traditional Inuit **culture** with that of the modern world.

Aglukark's songs have messages that ask for peace to come to all people. Some of her songs tell stories from her culture. They tell of daily life and survival in the far north.

Susan Aglukark was given the 2022 JUNO Humanitarian Award for her work improving the lives of young people in Northern Indigenous communities.

The Inuit Today

In the 1970s, Inuit living in Canada asked for a new territory so they could preserve their traditional way of life. On April 1, 1999, Canada's government created Nunavut (NOO-na-voot). It is a territory run by the Inuit.

Nunavut is nearly one million square miles (two million sq km). More than 31,000 Inuit live there. Nunavut is important to Inuit **culture**. It allows the Inuit living there to control their own affairs and have their own government.

Today, in Fairbanks, Alaska, many Inuit gather for the World Eskimo-Indian Olympics. The gathering consists of traditional songs, dances, and games. Some of the games include tug-o-war, the ear pull, and the blanket toss.

For the blanket toss, people hold on to a blanket and another person climbs on to the stretched blanket. That person is then tossed high into the air. The blanket toss was traditionally used by hunters to spot marine animals on the ice flows.

The blanket toss is also part of a festival called Nalukataq which means “to toss up.”

Glossary

banish—to force someone to leave his or her homelands.

blubber—a layer of fat in whales.

bow drill—a drill that has a long movable shaft with a stone point tip, a mouthpiece, and a bow. The drill is held in the mouth, and a bow is moved across the shaft. This turns the shaft so the tip can bore holes.

culture—the customs, arts, and tools of a nation or people at a certain time.

driftwood—wood that drifts on water or is washed ashore by water.

endanger—in danger of becoming extinct.

harpoon—a long spear, made from driftwood or whale bone, used to kill seals, walruses, and whales.

hide—an animal skin that is often thick and heavy.

migrate—to move from one place to another.

sinew—a band of tough fibers that joins a muscle to a bone.

sod—a piece of grass, usually cut into a strip and held together by roots.

umiak—a large boat that was about 20 to 30 feet (6 to 9 m) in length, 8 feet wide (2 m), and 3 feet (1 m) deep. The frame was made from driftwood covered with walrus hides. It was steered with paddles.

ONLINE RESOURCES

To learn more about the Inuit, please visit **abdobooklinks.com** or scan this QR code. These links are routinely monitored and updated to provide the most current information available.

Index